E Nye
Nye, Christopher
The old shepherd's tale /
2106

34028058847733
TOM$16.95 ocm56960695

3 4028 05884 7733
HARRIS COUNTY PUBLIC LIBRARY

D1201970

The Old Shepherd's Tale

To the one whose telling
became this story

HOUSATONIC PRESS
187 Main Street, Great Barrington, MA 01230
www.myrin.org/hp

Copyright ©2004 Housatonic Press. All rights reserved.

First Edition

Printed in Singapore by C. S. Graphics

Designed by Hans Teensma/Impress, Inc.

ISBN 0-913098-85-X

The Old Shepherd's Tale

CHRISTOPHER NYE

ILLUSTRATED BY HENRI SØRENSEN

HOUSATONIC PRESS

4

I N THE OLD DAYS it was different with the animals. When humankind had not yet invented the machinery we have today, children watched over herds of goats and cows as they grazed; men labored all day with strong oxen; women made clothing from sheep's wool, and made butter and cheese from cow's milk. People and good creatures like these spent so much time together that they understood each other. Everyone knew that these animals were helpful, and very important for human life.

So it was on the night of Jesus' birth in Bethlehem that animals played a special part. You have heard the story of how there was no room at the inn, and how Mary and Joseph had to sleep in the stable. Another story tells about the ox, the donkey, and the cow, and the old shepherd who took care of them.

For the ox it had been a hard day, dragging loads of stones out of a farmer's field. For the donkey it had been a hard day too, carrying firewood into town from the hills. For the cow it had been a day of milk-making, like most days — eating hay, chewing her cud, and dreaming of the green pastures that would come in spring.

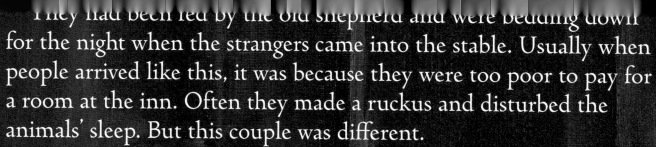

They had been led by the old shepherd and were bedding down for the night when the strangers came into the stable. Usually when people arrived like this, it was because they were too poor to pay for a room at the inn. Often they made a ruckus and disturbed the animals' sleep. But this couple was different.

The man was kindly and quiet. He carried a lantern and helped the young woman, who held his arm. She seemed tired from traveling and it was clear that she would soon give birth. In her face there was an expression even the animals sensed — patient and accepting.

The two seemed surprised to find the old shepherd there.

He explained that he cared for the animals; and on nights like this when it was too cold for his old bones to be out under the stars, he slept in the stable. And cold it was. Even with the heat from the animals, you could see your breath inside.

After some further exchange of words in the manner of humans, the couple spread their blankets on some hay, the light went out, and everyone fell asleep.

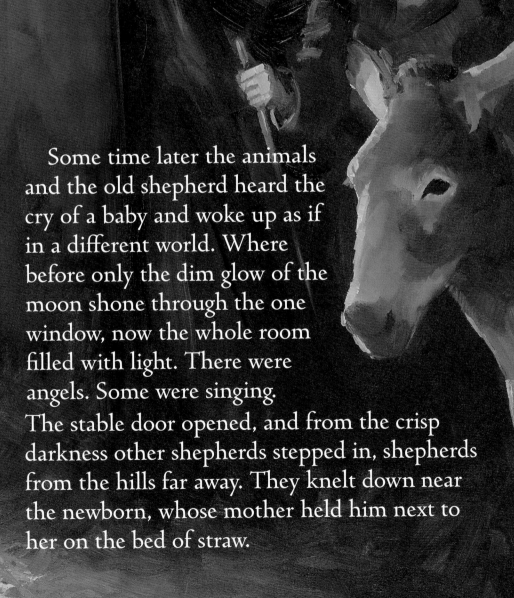

Some time later the animals and the old shepherd heard the cry of a baby and woke up as if in a different world. Where before only the dim glow of the moon shone through the one window, now the whole room filled with light. There were angels. Some were singing.
The stable door opened, and from the crisp darkness other shepherds stepped in, shepherds from the hills far away. They knelt down near the newborn, whose mother held him next to her on the bed of straw.

Suddenly all fell silent. From the hush an angel spoke in a voice that sounded out like a bell.

"The birth of this child will bring the greatest changes on earth, even into the distant future."

13

Then the angel turned back to the child. The donkey shook his head so that his long ears flapped. He blinked his eyes.

"Am I dreaming?" he asked aloud.

"No," said the cow. "I know about dreaming, and this is not a dream."

"But isn't it strange that we can speak to each other, just at this

time?" the ox added. They looked over toward the newborn and saw an understanding smile in the face of the mother as her gaze met theirs.

"Listen," said the cow, "this baby has no crib."

"Our manger," said the ox, "that will make a good crib."

15

"Yes," responded the donkey, and he moved over to the couple. "Here," he said, addressing the father directly and pointing with his nose to the manger. "If you clean out that old hay and add fresh, you can make a little bed."

Joseph proceeded to do this, but as he was picking up some fresh hay the donkey stopped him.

"No, not that —" said the donkey.

16

The cow interrupted. "This child should have the special hay they feed us on the Sabbath." She extended her nose toward a section of the hayloft overhead.

The ox nodded his approval and soon Joseph brought a soft, sweet-smelling clover and prepared the manger as a crib. When Mary placed Jesus in it, he went right to sleep. Before long all the angels but one disappeared, the bright light was gone, and in the stillness all fell asleep again.

Along toward morning but before the sun's fingers reached over the horizon, the animals began speaking softly among themselves. Each of them had dreamed pictures that foretold gifts they or animals of their kind would make to this child in years to come, gifts that would help him in his difficult life.

The cow explained, "My gift will be milk and food made from milk that nourishes the human body. With this he can grow into a healthy man."

The donkey explained, "My gift will be protection from danger. I saw in my dream a donkey like myself carrying the mother and babe into Egypt, a land that will shield him from the darkest danger."

The ox explained, "My gift will be strength. In my dream I saw him grown up as a carpenter and able to lift big timbers and the heavy cross he will one day carry."

Awakened again, the old shepherd was amazed. He had already marveled that the animals could talk on this sacred night, a night of angels, a night of miracles. Now he stood in awe to hear the wisdom coming through these animals, his friends, and it made him love and appreciate them all the more. In the bright days and dark nights that followed, he carried these moments like secrets close to his heart.

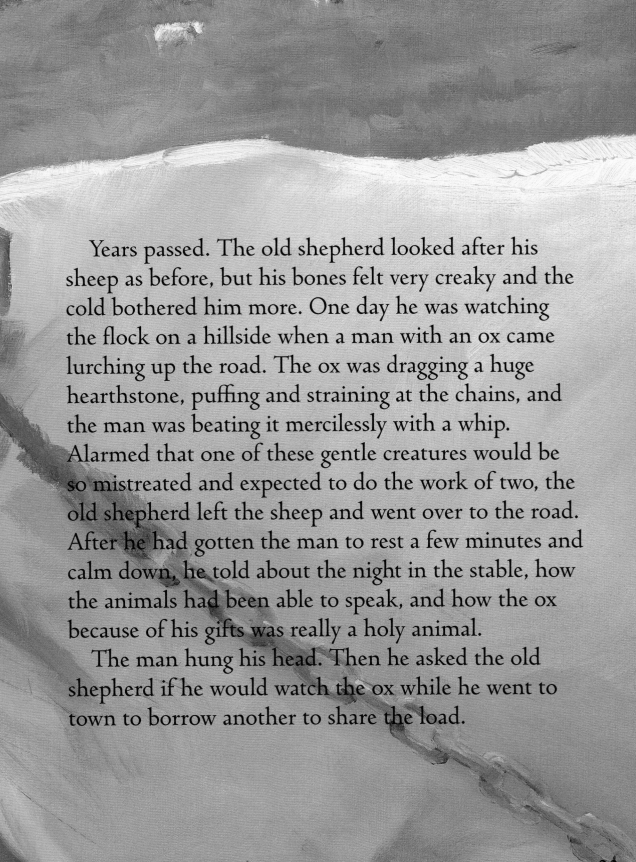

Years passed. The old shepherd looked after his sheep as before, but his bones felt very creaky and the cold bothered him more. One day he was watching the flock on a hillside when a man with an ox came lurching up the road. The ox was dragging a huge hearthstone, puffing and straining at the chains, and the man was beating it mercilessly with a whip. Alarmed that one of these gentle creatures would be so mistreated and expected to do the work of two, the old shepherd left the sheep and went over to the road. After he had gotten the man to rest a few minutes and calm down, he told about the night in the stable, how the animals had been able to speak, and how the ox because of his gifts was really a holy animal.

The man hung his head. Then he asked the old shepherd if he would watch the ox while he went to town to borrow another to share the load.

Another day the old shepherd passed by a yard and saw two donkeys that were almost starving. He tracked down the drunken owner, carousing with his friends nearby. But he saw that this man would never take proper care of his animals so the old shepherd bought them, took them away, and grazed them with his sheep until they were healthy again. Then he sold them to a good-hearted family who would treat them well.

One evening after dark when he returned to the stable, the old shepherd found the cow, the very same one with whom he had shared the night of miracles. She was in great pain and shifted her weight from one hoof to another. Her udder seemed full enough to burst. Normally the cow was milked by a maid from the inn, but she had gone off to town with a young man. The shepherd found a bucket and set about milking.

When the girl returned later, they had a talk. She already knew that a special birth had occurred right there in the stable, but she had heard nothing about the animals' part in it. The old man explained how painful it is for a cow not to be milked. He also told how the animals gave up their manger, of the gifts they had foreseen, and of the patient, dreamy gentleness of this one who stood before them.

The girl cried because she really loved the cow and had never meant to hurt her. She had been thoughtless, but she never forgot again.

27

And it came to pass in the old shepherd's last days, as he felt his strength for this life ebb away, he realized that ever since he was a child he had been with animals more than people. He regretted this not at all because he enjoyed serving their simple needs for water, for food or fresh pasture, for protection.

But one question troubled him and would not let him rest. The animals at Jesus' birth, they appeared so humble, and yet there was a greatness in them. Other people did not see this. When they saw an ox, they recognized only his size and strength. When they saw a donkey resting under a tree along the dusty roads, they saw only a beast of burden. For them a cow meant only milk. The shepherd saw much more. Why was this so? Was he just a foolish old man imagining things? He prayed that before he died he could know the answer to his question.

The final hour approached. He had said good-bye to his friends. It was evening and he had been dozing. He wakened and as he opened his eyes, the wall of the room seemed to fall away. In its place stood an angel. It spoke.

"I have come to answer your question." Suddenly the shepherd was as alert as a bird. "When you were present in the stable at the birth of him who will come to be called The Good Shepherd, what you saw and heard laid a seed in your heart, a seed that grew into love for these animals and all of their kind. You remained true to that seed, and we thank you for your love and faithfulness to creatures who cannot speak out for themselves.

"The oxen, the donkeys, and the cows, and the higher beings that stand behind each group, received a blessing on that night, and particular powers. From that time and deep into the future their life forces will be shared with the entire human race — strength from the ox, protection from the donkey, nourishment from the cow. It is important to value these animals as they deserve. They will have very special tasks in the distance of time, to the extent that animals can help at all."

The angel paused for a moment. When it spoke again, the voice was soft and echoing as if from a great distance.

"Human beings may do as they wish, but they should know they only hurt themselves if they do not see how very useful these three animals are. Whoever despises these holy animals will be able to have but little of their forces."

Slowly the image of the angel vanished. The shepherd felt himself filled with wonder and gratitude and peace.